Trading Mastery:

Unleashing Financial Potential in the Modern Markets Innovative Strategies, Prudent Approaches, and Insider insights for Mastering the Art of Trading

By
GEORGE L. BROWN

© Copyright 2023 by - GEORGE L . BROWN - All rights reserved. This document is geared towards providing exact and reliable information in regards to the topic and issue covered. The publication is sold with the idea that the publisher is not required to render accounting, officially permitted, or otherwise, qualified services. If advice is necessary, legal or professional, a practiced individual in the profession should be ordered. - From a Declaration of Principles which was accepted and approved equally by a Committee of the American Bar Association and a Committee of Publishers and Associations. In no way is it legal to reproduce, duplicate, or transmit any part of this document in either electronic means or in printed format. Recording of this publication is strictly prohibited and any storage of this document is not allowed unless with written permission from the publisher. All rights reserved. The information provided herein is stated to be truthful and consistent, in that any liability, in terms of inattention or otherwise, by any usage or abuse of any policies, processes, or directions contained within is the solitary and utter responsibility of the recipient reader. Under no circumstances will any legal responsibility or blame be held against the publisher for any reparation, damages, or monetary loss due to the information herein, either directly or indirectly.

Respective authors own all copyrights not held by the publisher. The information herein is offered for informational purposes solely, and is universal as so. The presentation of the information is without contract or any type of guarantee assurance.

The trademarks that are used are without any consent, and the publication of the trademark is without permission or backing by the trademark owner. All trademarks and brands within this book are for clarifying purposes only and are the owned by the owners themselves, not affiliated with this document.

CONTENTS

INTRODUCTION: 9

CHAPTER 1: "THE WORLD'S GREATEST OPPORTUNITY MACHINE: UNLOCKING YOUR PATH TO PROFIT" 11

    INTRODUCTION: 11
    PARAGRAPH 1: UNDERSTANDING THE OPPORTUNITY 11
    PARAGRAPH 2: RESEARCH AND EDUCATION 12
    PARAGRAPH 3: BUILDING A STRONG NETWORK 12
    PARAGRAPH 4: DEVELOPING A STRATEGIC PLAN 13
    PARAGRAPH 5: IMPLEMENTATION AND MONITORING 13
    PARAGRAPH 6: EMBRACING ADAPTABILITY AND CONTINUOUS LEARNING 13
    CONCLUSION: 14
    NOTE: 14

CHAPTER 2: "HOW TO GET STARTED WITH STOCKS: A COMPREHENSIVE GUIDE TO MAXIMIZING YOUR PROFIT POTENTIAL" 15

    INTRODUCTION: 15
    PARAGRAPH 1: UNDERSTANDING THE STOCK MARKET 15
    PARAGRAPH 2: CLARIFYING YOUR INVESTMENT GOALS 16
    PARAGRAPH 3: CONDUCTING THOROUGH RESEARCH 16
    PARAGRAPH 4: BUILDING A DIVERSIFIED PORTFOLIO 17
    PARAGRAPH 5: OPENING A BROKERAGE ACCOUNT 17
    PARAGRAPH 6: DEVELOPING A COMPREHENSIVE INVESTMENT STRATEGY 18
    PARAGRAPH 7: MONITORING AND REVIEWING YOUR PORTFOLIO REGULARLY 18
    PARAGRAPH 8: EMBRACING A LONG-TERM PERSPECTIVE 19
    PARAGRAPH 9: CONTINUING EDUCATION AND LEARNING 19
    PARAGRAPH 10: SEEKING PROFESSIONAL ADVICE 20
    CONCLUSION: 20

CHAPTER 3: "MAKE MONEY WITH ETFS: UNLOCKING PROFIT POTENTIAL WITH CAUTION" 21

    INTRODUCTION: 21
    PARAGRAPH 1: UNDERSTANDING ETFS 21
    PARAGRAPH 2: DEFINING YOUR INVESTMENT GOALS 22
    PARAGRAPH 3: RESEARCHING ETFS 22
    PARAGRAPH 4: UNDERSTANDING INDEX-BASED AND ACTIVELY MANAGED ETFS ... 22
    PARAGRAPH 5: ASSESSING COSTS AND FEES 23
    PARAGRAPH 6: DIVERSIFYING YOUR ETF PORTFOLIO 23
    PARAGRAPH 7: OPENING A BROKERAGE ACCOUNT 24
    PARAGRAPH 8: IMPLEMENTING A SYSTEMATIC INVESTMENT PLAN 24

PARAGRAPH 9: MONITORING AND REVIEWING YOUR ETF PORTFOLIO 24
PARAGRAPH 10: SEEKING PROFESSIONAL GUIDANCE 25
CONCLUSION: 25

CHAPTER 4: "CREATING PASSIVE INCOME WITH DIVIDEND STOCKS: UNLEASHING THE CREATIVE POWER OF INVESTMENT" 27

INTRODUCTION: 27
PARAGRAPH 1: UNDERSTANDING DIVIDEND STOCKS 27
PARAGRAPH 2: DEFINING YOUR PASSIVE INCOME GOALS 28
PARAGRAPH 3: RESEARCHING DIVIDEND-PAYING COMPANIES 28
PARAGRAPH 4: BUILDING A DIVERSIFIED DIVIDEND STOCK PORTFOLIO 29
PARAGRAPH 5: EVALUATING DIVIDEND YIELD AND DIVIDEND GROWTH 29
PARAGRAPH 6: ASSESSING DIVIDEND PAYOUT RATIO AND FINANCIAL HEALTH 29
PARAGRAPH 7: REINVESTING DIVIDENDS FOR COMPOUND GROWTH 30
PARAGRAPH 8: MONITORING AND ADJUSTING YOUR DIVIDEND PORTFOLIO 30
PARAGRAPH 9: EXPLORING DIVIDEND ETFS AND FUNDS 31
PARAGRAPH 10: SEEKING PROFESSIONAL GUIDANCE 31
CONCLUSION: 32

CHAPTER 5: "UNLEASHING YOUR INNER WARREN BUFFETT: MASTERING THE ART OF STOCK SELECTION WITH CREATIVITY AND CAUTION" 33

INTRODUCTION: 33
PARAGRAPH 1: STUDY THE PRINCIPLES OF WARREN BUFFETT 33
PARAGRAPH 2: DEFINE YOUR INVESTMENT OBJECTIVES 34
PARAGRAPH 3: RESEARCH AND ANALYZE COMPANIES 34
PARAGRAPH 4: ASSESS THE MANAGEMENT TEAM 35
PARAGRAPH 5: UNDERSTAND THE MOAT 35
PARAGRAPH 6: ANALYZE VALUATION METRICS 35
PARAGRAPH 7: CONDUCT A MARGIN OF SAFETY ANALYSIS 36
PARAGRAPH 8: EMBRACE A LONG-TERM MINDSET 36
PARAGRAPH 9: DIVERSIFY YOUR PORTFOLIO 36
PARAGRAPH 10: STAY INFORMED AND CONTINUOUSLY LEARN 37
CONCLUSION: 37

CHAPTER 6: "UNLEASHING THE POWER OF VALUE INVESTING: EXPLORING P/E RATIOS WITH CREATIVITY AND CAUTION" 39

INTRODUCTION: 39
PARAGRAPH 1: UNDERSTANDING VALUE INVESTING 39
PARAGRAPH 2: THE SIGNIFICANCE OF P/E RATIOS 40
PARAGRAPH 3: RESEARCHING AND SELECTING INDUSTRIES 41
PARAGRAPH 4: IDENTIFYING POTENTIAL VALUE STOCKS 42
PARAGRAPH 5: ASSESSING P/E RATIO TRENDS 43
PARAGRAPH 6: CONDUCTING IN-DEPTH FUNDAMENTAL ANALYSIS 44
PARAGRAPH 7: CONSIDERING QUALITATIVE FACTORS 45

PARAGRAPH 8: PRACTICING CAUTION AND RISK MANAGEMENT 47
PARAGRAPH 9: EMBRACING CREATIVITY AND INNOVATION 48
PARAGRAPH 10: EXERCISING CAUTION AND DUE DILIGENCE 49
IN CONCLUSION 50

CHAPTER 7: MAKE MONEY WITH GROWTH STOCKS 51

PARAGRAPH 1: UNDERSTANDING GROWTH STOCKS AND THEIR POTENTIAL 51
PARAGRAPH 2: IDENTIFYING PROMISING GROWTH COMPANIES 52
PARAGRAPH 3: ASSESSING GROWTH POTENTIAL 53
PARAGRAPH 4: MANAGING RISKS ASSOCIATED WITH GROWTH STOCKS 53
PARAGRAPH 5: INVESTING WITH CAUTION 54
PARAGRAPH 6: INVESTING IN HIGH-GROWTH SECTORS 55
PARAGRAPH 7: GROWTH STOCKS AS A PORTFOLIO COMPONENT 56
CONCLUSION: 56

CHAPTER 8: MAKE MONEY WITH IPOS 58

INTRODUCTION: 58
PARAGRAPH 1: UNDERSTANDING IPOS AND THEIR POTENTIAL 58
PARAGRAPH 2: RESEARCHING IPO CANDIDATES 59
PARAGRAPH 3: EVALUATING IPO PRICING AND VALUATION 59
PARAGRAPH 4: ASSESSING THE IPO ROADSHOW AND INVESTOR SENTIMENT 60
PARAGRAPH 5: TIMING AND ALLOCATION STRATEGY 61
PARAGRAPH 6: MANAGING RISKS AND SETTING REALISTIC EXPECTATIONS 61
PARAGRAPH 7: LONG-TERM INVESTMENT APPROACH 62
PARAGRAPH 8: REGULAR PORTFOLIO MONITORING AND REASSESSMENT 63
CONCLUSION: 63

CHAPTER 9: HOW TO PROFIT FROM A STOCK THAT IS GOING NOWHERE 65

INTRODUCTION: 65
PARAGRAPH 1: UNDERSTANDING STOCKS WITH LIMITED PRICE MOVEMENT 65
PARAGRAPH 2: CONDUCTING THOROUGH FUNDAMENTAL ANALYSIS 66
PARAGRAPH 3: IDENTIFYING POTENTIAL CATALYSTS 66
PARAGRAPH 4: UTILIZING OPTIONS STRATEGIES 67
PARAGRAPH 5: IMPLEMENTING A RANGE-TRADING STRATEGY 68
PARAGRAPH 6: EMPLOYING CONTRARIAN INVESTING APPROACHES 68
PARAGRAPH 7: LEVERAGING TECHNICAL ANALYSIS TOOLS 69
PARAGRAPH 8: MONITORING NEWS AND MARKET TRENDS 69
CONCLUSION: 70

CHAPTER 10: A DAY TRADING STRATEGY THAT ACTUALLY WORKS 72

INTRODUCTION: 72
PARAGRAPH 1: UNDERSTANDING THE MARKET AND DEFINING YOUR TRADING GOALS 72
PARAGRAPH 2: CONDUCTING THOROUGH TECHNICAL ANALYSIS 73
PARAGRAPH 3: UTILIZING CANDLESTICK PATTERNS FOR TIMING ENTRIES 73

- Paragraph 4: Implementing a Robust Risk Management Strategy 73
- Paragraph 5: Identifying High-Volume and Volatile Stocks 74
- Paragraph 6: Utilizing Market Depth and Level II Data 74
- Paragraph 7: Developing a Scalping Strategy for Quick Profits 75
- Paragraph 8: Practicing Trade Journaling and Performance Review 75
- Paragraph 9: Continuous Learning and Adaptation 76
- Conclusion: 76

CHAPTER 11: FIVE HUGE MISTAKES THAT BEGINNERS MAKE 77

- Introduction: 77
- Paragraph 1: Lack of Research and Due Diligence 77
- Paragraph 2: Emotional Decision-Making 78
- Paragraph 3: Lack of Diversification 78
- Paragraph 4: Chasing Quick Returns and Fads 79
- Paragraph 5: Ignoring Risk Management 79
- Paragraph 6: Overlooking the Power of Compounding 80
- Paragraph 7: Neglecting Continuous Education 80
- Paragraph 8: Failing to Maintain a Long-Term Perspective 81
- Paragraph 9: Seeking Professional Guidance 81
- Conclusion: 82

CHAPTER 12: INSIDER SECRETS OF THE STOCK MARKET 83

- Introduction: 83
- Paragraph 1: Fundamental Analysis and Research 83
- Paragraph 2: Technical Analysis and Chart Patterns 84
- Paragraph 3: Risk Management and Position Sizing 84
- Paragraph 4: Market Timing and Entry Points 85
- Paragraph 5: Developing a Winning Strategy 85
- Paragraph 6: Continual Learning and Adaptability 85
- Paragraph 7: Patience and Long-Term Perspective 86
- Paragraph 8: Managing Emotions and Avoiding Herd Mentality 86
- Paragraph 9: Harnessing the Power of Technology and Data 88
- Paragraph 10: Building a Network and Seeking Mentorship 88
- Conclusion: 89

CHAPTER 13: FROM SMALL BEGINNERS TO GREAT WEALTH 90

- Introduction: 90
- Paragraph 1: Defining Your Financial Goals 90
- Paragraph 2: Assessing Your Risk Tolerance 91
- Paragraph 3: Building a Diversified Portfolio 91
- Paragraph 4: Conducting In-Depth Investment Research 91
- Paragraph 5: Embracing a Long-Term Perspective 92
- Paragraph 6: Regular Portfolio Reviews and Adjustments 92
- Paragraph 7: Optimizing Tax-Efficient Strategies 92

PARAGRAPH 8: SEEKING PROFESSIONAL GUIDANCE 93
PARAGRAPH 9: EMBRACING INNOVATION AND EMERGING TRENDS 93
PARAGRAPH 10: PRACTICING PATIENCE, DISCIPLINE, AND CONTINUOUS LEARNING 93
PARAGRAPH 11: CULTIVATING A SAVINGS HABIT 94
PARAGRAPH 12: NETWORK AND COLLABORATE 94
PARAGRAPH 13: KEEP UP WITH ECONOMIC INDICATORS 94
PARAGRAPH 14: HARNESS THE POWER OF COMPOUNDING 95
PARAGRAPH 15: ADOPT A MINDFUL APPROACH 95
PARAGRAPH 16: STAY EDUCATED AND ADAPTABLE 95
PARAGRAPH 17: SEEK MULTIPLE INCOME STREAMS 96
PARAGRAPH 18: PRACTICE RISK MANAGEMENT 96
CONCLUSION: 97

CONCLUSION: 98

Introduction:

Welcome to the captivating realm of trading, where financial opportunities abound and the thrill of making strategic decisions shapes your path to prosperity. In this innovative and creatively inspired book, we embark on an exhilarating journey through the world of trading, catering to men and women between the ages of 30 and 50 who are venturing into this realm for the very first time.

Gone are the days when trading was confined to Wall Street tycoons in suits and ties. Today, trading has become an accessible and empowering endeavor, embracing individuals from all walks of life. It's time to break free from the conventional stereotypes and explore the limitless possibilities that await you in the world of finance.

In "Trading Mastery: Unleashing Your Creative Edge in the Financial Markets," we redefine the way you approach trading. We infuse it with a touch of creativity and innovation, allowing you to harness your unique talents and perspectives to succeed in this dynamic landscape. Whether you're an artist, a writer, an engineer, or a marketer, you'll discover that your creative skills can be powerfully translated into the realm of trading.

This book is not your typical dry and technical guide. Instead, we take you on a stimulating journey where imagination meets numbers, where analysis dances with intuition, and where risk management becomes an art form. Drawing upon the wisdom of seasoned traders and innovative thinkers, we blend practical strategies with unconventional approaches, empowering you to develop your own trading style that aligns with your passions and strengths.

As you delve deeper into the pages of "Trading Mastery," you'll uncover a wealth of knowledge, from understanding the fundamental principles of trading to mastering advanced strategies. We demystify complex concepts, employing a conversational tone that makes the information accessible and relatable. Moreover, we provide valuable insights into the psychological aspects of trading, helping you navigate the emotional rollercoaster that accompanies financial markets.

So, whether you aspire to supplement your income, secure your financial future, or simply indulge in a thrilling new adventure, "Trading Mastery" will equip you with the tools, techniques, and creative mindset necessary to thrive in the trading world. Prepare to embark on a transformative journey that will forever change the way you view the intersection of artistry and finance.

Are you ready to unleash your creative edge and master the art of trading? Let's embark on this exhilarating adventure together, and unlock the hidden potential that lies within you.

Note: Please keep in mind that trading involves significant risks, and individuals should conduct thorough research and seek professional advice before engaging in any financial activities.

Chapter 1: "The World's Greatest Opportunity Machine: Unlocking Your Path to Profit"

Introduction:

Welcome to the remarkable world of "The World's Greatest Opportunity Machine." In this chapter, we will explore a transformative opportunity that has the potential to propel your earnings to new heights. With a strategic approach and the right mindset, you can tap into this extraordinary machine and pave the way for financial success. So, fasten your seatbelts and get ready to embark on a thrilling journey toward limitless possibilities.

Paragraph 1: Understanding the Opportunity

To begin this exhilarating venture, it's crucial to understand the opportunity at hand. "The World's Greatest Opportunity Machine" operates on the principle of leveraging emerging market trends and technological advancements. It provides a platform for investors to capitalize on lucrative opportunities and reap substantial financial rewards. By staying informed about market shifts, disruptive innovations, and global economic trends, you can position yourself to seize this remarkable opportunity.

Paragraph 2: Research and Education

Education is the key to unlocking the full potential of "The World's Greatest Opportunity Machine." Engage in thorough research to gain a deep understanding of the market and its dynamics. Study successful investment strategies, learn about risk management techniques, and delve into the intricacies of the specific area where this opportunity lies. Equip yourself with knowledge, attend seminars, read books, and engage with experts to expand your expertise.

Paragraph 3: Building a Strong Network

In the world of investment, a strong network can be invaluable. Surround yourself with like-minded individuals who are also exploring "The World's Greatest Opportunity Machine." Connect with experienced investors, attend industry events, and join online communities to exchange ideas, share insights, and gain valuable mentorship. Collaborating with a supportive network will amplify your understanding and enhance your chances of success.

Paragraph 4: Developing a Strategic Plan

Success in any venture requires a well-thought-out plan, and "The World's Greatest Opportunity Machine" is no exception. Craft a strategic plan that aligns with your financial goals, risk tolerance, and timeframe. Define your investment criteria, establish clear entry and exit strategies, and outline your risk management protocols. A well-defined plan will guide your actions and help you make informed decisions along the way.

Paragraph 5: Implementation and Monitoring

With your plan in hand, it's time to put it into action. Execute your investment strategy systematically, keeping a close eye on market trends and signals. Regularly monitor your investments, track performance, and make adjustments as needed. Stay disciplined and avoid impulsive decisions driven by market fluctuations. Patience

Paragraph 6: Embracing Adaptability and Continuous Learning

"The World's Greatest Opportunity Machine" is a dynamic and ever-evolving landscape. To navigate it successfully, you must embrace adaptability and prioritize continuous learning. Stay open to new ideas, remain flexible in your approach, and be willing to adapt your strategies as market conditions change. Engage in ongoing education, stay updated on industry news, and seek opportunities for personal and professional growth. The more you invest in your own knowledge and adaptability, the better equipped you'll be to capitalize on the ever-changing opportunities presented by this remarkable machine.

Conclusion:

"The World's Greatest Opportunity Machine" holds the potential to revolutionize your financial future. By understanding the opportunity, conducting thorough research, building a strong network, developing a strategic plan, implementing it diligently, and embracing adaptability, you can maximize your chances of success in this exciting endeavor. Remember, the path to profit may not always be smooth, but with dedication, perseverance, and a commitment to continuous learning, you can unlock the full potential of this extraordinary machine and pave the way to financial prosperity.

Note: It's essential to approach any investment opportunity with caution and conduct thorough due diligence. This chapter is intended to provide a general overview and should not be considered financial advice. Always seek the guidance of a qualified financial advisor before making any investment decisions.

Chapter 2: "How to Get Started with Stocks: A Comprehensive Guide to Maximizing Your Profit Potential"

Introduction:

Welcome to the thrilling world of stocks, where the potential for financial growth and wealth creation awaits. In this chapter, we will explore in detail the specific steps you need to take to navigate this opportunity and maximize your profit potential. Whether you're a seasoned investor or a novice looking to enter the market, this comprehensive guide will equip you with the knowledge and tools necessary to make informed decisions and achieve success.

Paragraph 1: Understanding the Stock Market

Before delving into the world of stocks, it's essential to gain a thorough understanding of the stock market. Familiarize yourself with the basic concepts such as stocks, shares, exchanges, and indices. Learn about the factors that influence stock prices, such as company performance, market trends, and economic indicators. This foundational knowledge will provide you with a solid understanding of how the stock market operates and the key drivers behind stock price movements.

Paragraph 2: Clarifying Your Investment Goals

To embark on your stock market journey, it's crucial to define your investment goals clearly and precisely. Are you seeking long-term growth, regular income, or a combination of both? Assess your risk tolerance and determine the timeframe for your investments. By establishing specific goals, you can craft an investment strategy that aligns with your desired outcomes and helps guide your decision-making process.

Paragraph 3: Conducting Thorough Research

Thorough research is paramount when venturing into the stock market. Dive deep into different industries, sectors, and companies that align with your investment goals. Analyze financial statements, annual reports, and news articles to gather insights about a company's performance, competitive position, and growth prospects. Study historical price data and identify trends that may influence stock prices. A solid research foundation will enable you to make well-informed investment decisions.

Paragraph 4: Building a Diversified Portfolio

Diversification is a crucial element in managing risk and maximizing your profit potential. Building a diversified portfolio involves investing in stocks from various industries, sectors, and market capitalizations. Consider incorporating different investment strategies, such as growth stocks, value stocks, and dividend-paying stocks. Diversifying your portfolio will help protect against volatility and position you for long-term success.

Paragraph 5: Opening a Brokerage Account

To invest in stocks, you'll need to open a brokerage account. Research reputable brokerage firms that align with your needs, considering factors such as fees, trading platforms, customer support, and research tools. Compare account options and complete the necessary paperwork to open your account. Take time to familiarize yourself with the trading platform, order types, and other essential features provided by your chosen brokerage. A reliable brokerage will facilitate smooth and efficient execution of your trades.

Paragraph 6: Developing a Comprehensive Investment Strategy

Crafting a comprehensive investment strategy is essential for navigating the stock market effectively. Consider your investment goals, risk tolerance, and time horizon when developing your strategy. Determine whether you'll be a passive investor, focusing on long-term growth, or an active trader, capitalizing on short-term market opportunities. Outline your criteria for selecting stocks, such as fundamental analysis, technical analysis, or a combination of both. Document your strategy and establish guidelines for portfolio rebalancing and risk management.

Paragraph 7: Monitoring and Reviewing Your Portfolio Regularly

Once you've invested in stocks, it's crucial to monitor and review your portfolio regularly. Stay informed about company news, economic indicators, and market trends that may impact your investments. Evaluate the performance of your stocks against your investment goals and adjust your portfolio as needed. Regularly review your investment strategy, taking into account new information and market conditions, to ensure it remains aligned with your objectives. Monitoring and reviewing your portfolio will enable you to make timely decisions and adapt to changes in the market, ultimately maximizing your profit potential.

Paragraph 8: Embracing a Long-Term Perspective

While the stock market can experience short-term fluctuations, it's essential to maintain a long-term perspective. Stocks have historically demonstrated the potential for significant growth over extended periods. Avoid being swayed by temporary market volatility and focus on the long-term value and potential of your investments. By staying committed to your investment strategy and weathering market cycles, you increase your chances of reaping the rewards of long-term stock ownership.

Paragraph 9: Continuing Education and Learning

The stock market is a dynamic and ever-evolving environment, and continued education is key to staying informed and making sound investment decisions. Stay up to date with industry news, economic trends, and investment strategies through books, online resources, seminars, and financial publications. Engage in discussions with fellow investors and seek insights from experienced professionals. A commitment to ongoing learning will help you navigate the complexities of the stock market and adapt to changing circumstances.

Paragraph 10: Seeking Professional Advice

While self-directed investing can be rewarding, seeking professional advice can provide valuable guidance and expertise. Consider consulting with a qualified financial advisor who can help you align your investment strategy with your goals and risk tolerance. A financial advisor can offer personalized recommendations, portfolio analysis, and help you navigate complex investment options. Their expertise and experience can provide you with an additional layer of confidence and peace of mind.

Conclusion:

Getting started with stocks requires a solid understanding of the stock market, clear investment goals, thorough research, diversification, opening a brokerage account, developing a comprehensive investment strategy, and regular portfolio monitoring. By embracing a long-term perspective, continuing education, and seeking professional advice when needed, you'll be well-positioned to navigate the stock market and maximize your profit potential. Remember, investing in stocks carries risks, and it's important to carefully assess your own financial situation and consult with professionals before making any investment decisions. With patience, discipline, and a commitment to ongoing learning, you can embark on a rewarding journey toward financial success in the stock market.

Chapter 3: "Make Money with ETFs: Unlocking Profit Potential with Caution"

Introduction:

Welcome to the exciting world of ETFs (Exchange-Traded Funds), where the potential for financial gain awaits. In this chapter, we will explore the specific steps you need to take to navigate this investment opportunity and maximize your profit potential. It is important to approach ETF investing with caution, as with any investment, but by following these steps and understanding the unique characteristics of ETFs, you can position yourself for success.

Paragraph 1: Understanding ETFs

To begin your journey into ETF investing, it is crucial to understand what ETFs are and how they work. ETFs are investment funds that trade on stock exchanges, representing a basket of assets such as stocks, bonds, or commodities. They offer diversification, flexibility, and cost efficiency compared to traditional mutual funds. Gain a solid understanding of the structure, benefits, and risks associated with ETFs before proceeding.

Paragraph 2: Defining Your Investment Goals

Clarify your investment goals before investing in ETFs. Determine whether you are seeking long-term growth, income, or a combination of both. Assess your risk tolerance and establish a timeframe for your investments. Defining clear investment goals will guide your selection of ETFs and help you align your investment strategy with your desired outcomes.

Paragraph 3: Researching ETFs

Conduct thorough research on different ETFs available in the market. Explore ETFs that align with your investment goals, asset class preferences, and geographical focus. Examine the underlying assets, expense ratios, performance history, and the fund's investment strategy. Evaluate the fund's tracking error and liquidity, as these factors can impact its performance and your ability to enter or exit positions efficiently.

Paragraph 4: Understanding Index-Based and Actively Managed ETFs

Different types of ETFs exist, including index-based and actively managed ETFs. Index-based ETFs aim to replicate the performance of a specific index, while actively managed ETFs are actively managed by a portfolio manager or team. Understand the differences between these types of ETFs and consider the investment approach that aligns with your investment goals and preferences.

Paragraph 5: Assessing Costs and Fees

Carefully assess the costs and fees associated with ETFs. Compare expense ratios, brokerage fees, and any other applicable charges. Lower expense ratios are generally preferred, as they can have a significant impact on your long-term returns. Consider the trade-offs between costs and the specific features or benefits offered by the ETF.

Paragraph 6: Diversifying Your ETF Portfolio

Diversification is key to managing risk in ETF investing. Build a diversified ETF portfolio by including a mix of asset classes, sectors, and geographic regions. Diversification can help reduce the impact of any single investment's performance on your overall portfolio. Allocate your investments strategically to achieve the desired balance between risk and potential return.

Paragraph 7: Opening a Brokerage Account

To invest in ETFs, you'll need to open a brokerage account. Research reputable brokerage firms that offer a wide range of ETFs, competitive commission fees, and user-friendly trading platforms. Consider factors such as customer support, research tools, and educational resources. Choose a brokerage that aligns with your needs and facilitates a smooth and secure investment process.

Paragraph 8: Implementing a Systematic Investment Plan

Consider implementing a systematic investment plan (SIP) when investing in ETFs. SIP involves regularly investing a fixed amount at predefined intervals, regardless of market conditions. This approach helps mitigate the impact of short-term market volatility and allows you to benefit from dollar-cost averaging. Set up automatic investments according to your financial capacity and investment goals.

Paragraph 9: Monitoring and Reviewing Your ETF Portfolio

Regularly monitor and review your ETF portfolio to ensure it remains aligned with your investment goals and market conditions. Stay informed about the performance of your

ETFs, any changes in their underlying assets or investment strategies, and market trends that may impact their performance. Evaluate your portfolio's diversification, risk exposure, and overall performance. Make adjustments as necessary to maintain a well-balanced and optimized portfolio.

Paragraph 10: Seeking Professional Guidance

ETF investing can be complex, and seeking professional guidance is advisable, especially if you are new to investing or unsure about certain aspects of ETFs. Consider consulting with a qualified financial advisor who specializes in ETF investing. A financial advisor can provide personalized advice, help you evaluate your investment goals and risk tolerance, and guide you in selecting the most suitable ETFs for your portfolio. Their expertise and experience can provide valuable insights and enhance your chances of success.

Conclusion:

Investing in ETFs can be a lucrative opportunity, but it requires careful consideration and understanding of the investment process. By understanding ETFs, defining your investment goals, conducting thorough research, assessing costs and fees, diversifying your ETF portfolio, opening a brokerage account, implementing a systematic investment plan, monitoring your portfolio, and seeking professional guidance when needed, you can navigate the world of ETF investing with caution and maximize your profit potential. Remember that investing involves risks, and it is important to assess your own financial situation and seek professional advice before making any investment decisions. With diligence, knowledge, and a cautious approach, you can unlock the profit potential offered by ETFs and work towards achieving your investment goals.

Chapter 4: "Creating Passive Income with Dividend Stocks: Unleashing the Creative Power of Investment"

Introduction:

Welcome to the exciting realm of creating passive income with dividend stocks. In this chapter, we will explore the specific steps you need to take to harness the creative and innovative potential of dividend stocks for generating steady income. With a cautious and strategic approach, dividend stocks can become a powerful tool for building wealth and achieving financial independence. Let's dive into the world of dividend investing and discover how to unlock its full potential.

Paragraph 1: Understanding Dividend Stocks

Before embarking on your journey of creating passive income with dividend stocks, it's essential to grasp the concept. Dividend stocks are shares of companies that distribute a portion of their earnings to shareholders in the form of regular dividends. These dividends provide investors with a steady stream of income on top of potential capital appreciation. Understand the characteristics, benefits, and risks associated with dividend stocks to make informed investment decisions.

Paragraph 2: Defining Your Passive Income Goals

To effectively utilize dividend stocks for generating passive income, you must define your income goals. Determine how much passive income you aim to receive and within what timeframe. Assess your risk tolerance and investment horizon to align your strategies with your objectives. By setting clear goals, you can tailor your dividend stock portfolio to meet your income needs.

Paragraph 3: Researching Dividend-Paying Companies

Thorough research is key to identifying high-quality dividend-paying companies. Look for established companies with a consistent track record of dividend payments and a history of increasing dividends over time. Assess the company's financial stability, profitability, and cash flow generation. Study their industry dynamics and competitive advantages. A well-researched selection of dividend-paying companies forms the foundation of your income-generating portfolio.

Paragraph 4: Building a Diversified Dividend Stock Portfolio

Diversification is crucial for managing risk and maximizing the potential of your dividend stock portfolio. Allocate your investments across different sectors, industries, and market caps. This diversification reduces the impact of any single stock's performance on your overall income stream. Aim for a mix of high-yield and dividend growth stocks to strike a balance between current income and future potential.

Paragraph 5: Evaluating Dividend Yield and Dividend Growth

When selecting dividend stocks, consider both the dividend yield and dividend growth potential. Dividend yield represents the annual dividend payment as a percentage of the stock's price. Look for stocks with a competitive yield relative to their industry peers. Additionally, assess the company's ability to increase its dividend payments over time, as this ensures your income stream keeps pace with inflation and grows in the long run.

Paragraph 6: Assessing Dividend Payout Ratio and Financial Health

Evaluate the dividend payout ratio and the financial health of the companies in your portfolio. The payout ratio indicates the proportion of earnings paid out as dividends. Seek companies with sustainable payout ratios, allowing them to continue paying dividends even during challenging economic conditions. Assess their balance sheet strength, debt levels, and cash flow generation to ensure the company can maintain dividend payments over time.

Paragraph 7: Reinvesting Dividends for Compound Growth

Consider reinvesting dividends to harness the power of compounding. Dividend reinvestment plans (DRIPs) allow you to automatically reinvest your dividends into additional shares of the same company. This compounding effect can significantly enhance your long-term returns and accelerate the growth of your passive income. Reinvesting dividends can be a creative way to continuously build wealth and increase your income over time.

Paragraph 8: Monitoring and Adjusting Your Dividend Portfolio

Regularly monitor the performance of your dividend stock portfolio and make adjustments when necessary. Stay informed about the financial health of the companies you own, changes in dividend policies, and industry trends. Evaluate the impact of external factors such as economic conditions, regulatory changes, and shifts in consumer behavior on your portfolio. Consider adjusting your holdings if a company's fundamentals deteriorate or if there are more attractive dividend opportunities available. Actively managing your dividend portfolio ensures that it remains optimized for generating passive income.

Paragraph 9: Exploring Dividend ETFs and Funds

Expand your dividend investing horizons by exploring dividend-focused exchange-traded funds (ETFs) and mutual funds. These investment vehicles provide diversification across multiple dividend-paying companies, saving you time and effort in selecting individual stocks. Research different dividend-focused ETFs and funds, comparing their performance, expense ratios, and investment strategies. Incorporating these instruments into your portfolio can enhance income generation and diversification.

Paragraph 10: Seeking Professional Guidance

Dividend investing can be complex, and seeking professional guidance can provide valuable insights and expertise. Consider consulting with a financial advisor specializing in dividend investing. A qualified advisor can help you evaluate your income goals, assess your risk tolerance, and guide you in selecting the most suitable dividend stocks and investment strategies. They can also provide ongoing monitoring and recommendations to optimize your portfolio's performance.

Conclusion:

Creating passive income with dividend stocks requires a strategic and cautious approach. By understanding dividend stocks, defining your passive income goals, researching dividend-paying companies, building a diversified portfolio, evaluating dividend yield and growth, assessing financial health, reinvesting dividends, monitoring and adjusting your portfolio, exploring dividend ETFs and funds, and seeking professional guidance when needed, you can unlock the creative and innovative power of dividend investing. Remember that investing involves risks, and it is crucial to assess your own financial situation, conduct thorough research, and consult with professionals before making any investment decisions. With diligence, creativity, and a cautious mindset, you can embark on a journey toward generating sustainable passive income with dividend stocks and achieving financial independence.

Chapter 5: "Unleashing Your Inner Warren Buffett: Mastering the Art of Stock Selection with Creativity and Caution"

Introduction:

Welcome to the world of investing where we explore the art of picking stocks like Warren Buffett. Warren Buffett, renowned investor and one of the most successful stock pickers of our time, has left behind a wealth of wisdom and insights that can guide us in our own investment journeys. In this chapter, we will delve into the specific steps you can take to maximize your potential for profit while embracing a creative and innovative approach. Remember, investing in stocks requires caution, and it's important to carefully assess your own financial situation before making any investment decisions.

Paragraph 1: Study the Principles of Warren Buffett

Begin your journey by studying the principles and investment philosophy of Warren Buffett. Understand his emphasis on value investing, seeking companies with strong competitive advantages, sound management, and attractive long-term prospects. Dive into his annual letters to shareholders, books, and interviews to gain insights into his investment approach and mindset.

Paragraph 2: Define Your Investment Objectives

Before picking stocks, clearly define your investment objectives. Determine whether you are seeking long-term growth, income, or a combination of both. Assess your risk tolerance and investment horizon. Defining your objectives will guide your stock selection process and help align your portfolio with your desired outcomes.

Paragraph 3: Research and Analyze Companies

Thoroughly research and analyze potential investment opportunities. Focus on companies with sustainable competitive advantages, robust financials, and favorable industry trends. Dive into their financial statements, annual reports, and industry research to understand their fundamentals, growth potential, and market positioning.

Paragraph 4: Assess the Management Team

Pay close attention to the management team of the companies you consider investing in. Look for experienced and trustworthy leaders who have a proven track record of creating value for shareholders. Assess their strategic vision, execution capabilities, and alignment with shareholder interests. A strong management team is a crucial factor in the long-term success of a company.

Paragraph 5: Understand the Moat

One of Warren Buffett's key concepts is the "economic moat." Seek companies with a sustainable competitive advantage or moat that protects their market position and profitability. This could be through strong brands, patents, cost advantages, or network effects. Understanding and investing in businesses with a wide moat can provide long-term stability and potential for growth.

Paragraph 6: Analyze Valuation Metrics

Evaluate the valuation metrics of the stocks you are considering. Look beyond just the stock price and consider metrics such as price-to-earnings ratio (P/E), price-to-book ratio (P/B), and dividend yield. Compare these metrics to historical averages, industry peers, and the overall market to assess whether the stock is undervalued or overvalued.

Paragraph 7: Conduct a Margin of Safety Analysis

Warren Buffett emphasizes the importance of having a margin of safety when investing. This means buying stocks at a significant discount to their intrinsic value to protect against potential downside risks. Conduct a thorough analysis of the company's fundamentals and future cash flows to estimate its intrinsic value and determine whether the current stock price offers an attractive margin of safety.

Paragraph 8: Embrace a Long-Term Mindset

Warren Buffett's success can largely be attributed to his long-term perspective on investments. Avoid being swayed by short-term market fluctuations and focus on the long-term potential of the companies you invest in. Invest in businesses you believe in and are willing to hold for the long haul, allowing compounding to work in your favor.

Paragraph 9: Diversify Your Portfolio

Diversification is a key strategy for managing risk in stock picking. Allocate your investments across different sectors, industries, and geographies. This spreads your risk and reduces the impact of any single investment

on your portfolio. Aim for a well-diversified portfolio that includes a mix of large-cap, mid-cap, and small-cap stocks. Diversification allows you to capture opportunities in different segments of the market while minimizing the impact of individual stock volatility.

Paragraph 10: Stay Informed and Continuously Learn

To pick stocks like Warren Buffett, it's essential to stay informed and continuously expand your knowledge. Keep up with the latest news, market trends, and industry developments that may impact your investments. Read financial publications, follow reputable investment blogs, and attend seminars or webinars to enhance your understanding of the stock market. Remember, investing is an ongoing learning process, and staying informed is crucial for making informed decisions.

Conclusion:

Picking stocks like Warren Buffett requires a unique blend of creativity, innovation, and caution. By studying Warren

Buffett's principles, defining your investment objectives, researching and analyzing companies, assessing management teams, understanding economic moats, analyzing valuation metrics, conducting margin of safety analysis, embracing a long-term mindset, diversifying your portfolio, and staying informed, you can unlock the potential for successful stock selection. Remember that investing involves risks, and it is important to carefully evaluate your own financial situation and consult with professionals before making any investment decisions. With a creative and cautious approach, you can navigate the stock market with confidence and work towards achieving your investment goals.

Chapter 6: "Unleashing the Power of Value Investing: Exploring P/E Ratios with Creativity and Caution"

Introduction:

Welcome to the exciting world of value investing and the utilization of price-to-earnings (P/E) ratios. In this chapter, we will delve into the specific steps you can take to harness the creative and innovative potential of value investing and effectively utilize P/E ratios as a tool for identifying investment opportunities. Value investing focuses on finding undervalued stocks in the market, presenting the potential for significant profit. However, it is important to approach investments with caution and carefully evaluate your own financial situation before making any investment decisions.

Paragraph 1: Understanding Value Investing

Value investing is an investment strategy that involves seeking stocks that are trading at a price lower than their intrinsic value. It aims to capitalize on market inefficiencies and identify companies that have been overlooked or undervalued by the broader market. Value investors analyze various fundamental factors to determine a stock's true worth and potential for long-term growth.

To effectively practice value investing, it is essential to understand the principles that guide this strategy. Key concepts include the importance of identifying intrinsic value, conducting thorough fundamental analysis, and having the patience to wait for the market to recognize the true worth of a stock. Value investing is about seeking out opportunities where the market has undervalued a company's potential, allowing investors to buy stocks at a discount.

Paragraph 2: The Significance of P/E Ratios

The price-to-earnings (P/E) ratio is a key metric used in value investing. It measures the price of a stock relative to its earnings per share (EPS). The P/E ratio provides insight into the market's perception of a company's future earnings potential. A low P/E ratio suggests that a stock may be undervalued, while a high P/E ratio indicates that it may be overvalued. Understanding and utilizing P/E ratios effectively can help identify attractive investment opportunities.

When analyzing a company's P/E ratio, it's important to consider both the historical and comparative aspects. Comparing a company's current P/E ratio to its historical average can provide insights into its valuation relative to its own past performance. Additionally, comparing the P/E ratios of similar companies within the industry can shed light on whether a stock is undervalued or overvalued in comparison to its peers.

It's crucial to remember that P/E ratios should not be viewed in isolation but rather in conjunction with other fundamental and qualitative factors. While a low P/E ratio may indicate potential value, it's essential to conduct further analysis to evaluate a company's financial health, growth prospects, and competitive advantage. A holistic approach to assessing P/E ratios will enable you to make well-informed investment decisions.

Paragraph 3: Researching and Selecting Industries

In value investing, it is crucial to research and select industries that are poised for growth or currently undervalued. Analyze industry trends, market dynamics, and competitive landscape. Look for industries with potential for disruption or undergoing a positive transformation. Identifying promising industries sets the foundation for identifying undervalued stocks within those sectors.

When selecting industries, consider macroeconomic factors that may impact their growth potential. Look for sectors that demonstrate long-term stability, resilience, and the potential for sustained growth. Conducting in-depth industry research, such as analyzing market reports, studying consumer behavior, and monitoring technological advancements, will help identify industries with strong fundamentals and promising future prospects.

Furthermore, stay informed about regulatory changes and evolving trends that may affect the chosen industries. This proactive approach to industry selection ensures that you focus your investment efforts in areas with the highest potential for value creation.

Paragraph 4: Identifying Potential Value Stocks

To identify potential value stocks, analyze individual companies within the selected industries. Look for companies with strong fundamentals, including consistent revenue growth, healthy profit margins, and low levels of debt. Evaluate their competitive advantages, management quality, and market positioning. Assess whether the company's current stock price is significantly lower than its intrinsic value.

One effective approach to identifying potential value stocks is to utilize fundamental analysis techniques. Dive deep into a company's financial statements, including its income statement, balance sheet, and cash flow statement. Pay attention to key financial metrics such as revenue growth, earnings stability, return on equity (ROE), and cash flow generation. These metrics provide insights into a company's financial health and its ability to generate sustainable profits.

Additionally, consider qualitative factors when evaluating potential value stocks. Assess the quality of the company's management team and their track record of executing successful strategies. Look for companies with a competitive advantage, such as a strong brand, unique product offering, or proprietary technology. Evaluate the company's ability to adapt to changing market conditions and seize growth opportunities.

By combining quantitative analysis with qualitative assessment, you can gain a comprehensive understanding of a company's value potential and determine whether it aligns with your investment objectives.

Paragraph 5: Assessing P/E Ratio Trends

When evaluating potential value stocks, assess the historical and current P/E ratio trends. Compare a company's P/E ratio to its historical average, as well as to the P/E ratios of its industry peers. A lower-than-average P/E ratio may indicate an undervalued stock. However, it's important to conduct further analysis and consider other factors alongside the P/E ratio to make informed investment decisions.

Consider the reasons behind a stock's low P/E ratio. Is it due to temporary market conditions or specific challenges faced by the company? Evaluate whether these factors are likely to be resolved or if they pose long-term risks. Additionally, compare the company's P/E ratio to its peers within the industry. A lower P/E ratio relative to its competitors could suggest that the stock is undervalued compared to similar companies in the market.

It's crucial to exercise caution when solely relying on P/E ratios for investment decisions. While a low P/E ratio may indicate value, it should be considered in the context of the company's overall financial health, growth prospects, and industry dynamics. Remember, value investing involves a comprehensive evaluation of various factors, and the P/E ratio is just one piece of the puzzle.

Paragraph 6: Conducting In-Depth Fundamental Analysis

In value investing, conducting in-depth fundamental analysis is crucial. Dive deep into a company's financial statements, annual reports, and other relevant sources of information. Evaluate key financial metrics such as revenue growth, earnings stability, return on equity, and cash flow generation. Look for signs of undervaluation that may not be apparent based on P/E ratios alone.

During the fundamental analysis process, pay attention to the company's competitive position within its industry. Assess the strength of its products or services, market share, and ability to adapt to changing consumer preferences. Evaluate the company's management team and their track record of driving growth and creating shareholder value.

Additionally, consider the company's growth prospects. Analyze its expansion plans, research and development efforts, and potential for entering new markets. Assess the industry's growth potential and the company's ability to capture a significant portion of that growth.

By conducting thorough fundamental analysis, you can gain a deep understanding of a company's financial health, competitive position, and growth potential. This analysis will help you identify value stocks that have the potential to deliver significant returns over the long term.

Paragraph 7: Considering Qualitative Factors

While P/E ratios provide quantitative insights, it is equally important to consider qualitative factors when assessing value stocks. Evaluate a company's competitive position, its management team's track record, and the potential for future growth or expansion. Consider macroeconomic factors such as industry trends, regulatory environment, and technological advancements that may impact the company's performance.

When considering qualitative factors, assess the company's competitive advantage or unique selling proposition. Does the company possess a strong brand reputation, intellectual property, or innovative capabilities that give it an edge over competitors? A sustainable competitive advantage can contribute to long-term value creation.

Evaluate the quality and track record of the company's management team. Look for experienced leaders with a proven ability to execute strategies, make prudent decisions, and navigate through challenges. Strong leadership plays a crucial role in driving a company's success and creating shareholder value.

Consider the company's growth potential and its ability to adapt to changing market dynamics. Assess whether the company is positioned to capitalize on emerging trends, technologies, or consumer preferences. Look for companies that demonstrate a culture of innovation and a willingness to invest in research and development to stay ahead of the competition.

Furthermore, consider the company's financial stability and risk management practices. Assess the level of debt, liquidity, and cash flow generation. A company with a strong balance sheet and efficient capital allocation is better equipped to withstand economic downturns and seize growth opportunities.

By considering qualitative factors alongside quantitative analysis, you can gain a holistic understanding of a company's value potential. This comprehensive approach allows you to make informed investment decisions that align with your investment goals and risk tolerance.

Paragraph 8: Practicing Caution and Risk Management

Value investing, like any investment strategy, requires caution and diligent risk management. While the goal is to identify undervalued stocks with significant upside potential, it's essential to be aware of the risks involved.

Diversify your portfolio across different industries and sectors to mitigate risk. This diversification strategy helps spread risk and reduces the impact of any single investment's performance on your overall portfolio. By investing in a variety of companies, you can potentially offset losses in some stocks with gains in others.

Set realistic expectations and avoid excessive speculation. Value investing focuses on long-term growth and may require patience as the market recognizes the true value of a stock. Avoid chasing short-term trends or getting swayed by market noise. Stay disciplined and stick to your investment strategy.

Regularly monitor your investments and stay updated on market trends and company-specific news. Keep track of the stocks you own and their performance. Periodically reassess the intrinsic value of your holdings and make adjustments if necessary. Be prepared to sell stocks that no longer meet your investment criteria or if the market conditions change significantly.

Remember, investing involves risks, and there are no guarantees of returns. Be cautious when allocating your capital and consider consulting with a financial advisor who can provide personalized guidance based on your individual circumstances and investment goals.

Paragraph 9: Embracing Creativity and Innovation

Value investing is not just about numbers and financial analysis; it also requires a creative and innovative mindset. Look beyond the surface and think outside the box when evaluating investment opportunities. Consider emerging industries, disruptive technologies, and changing consumer behaviors that may present unique value investment prospects.

Stay updated with market trends and advancements in investment strategies. Explore innovative approaches to value investing, such as using artificial intelligence and machine learning algorithms to identify undervalued stocks. Embrace new tools and technologies that can enhance your investment research and decision-making process.

In addition, seek inspiration from successful investors and their strategies. Study the methods of renowned value investors like Warren Buffett, Benjamin Graham, and Charlie Munger. Understand their principles and adapt them to your own investment approach, incorporating your unique insights and perspectives.

By infusing creativity and innovation into your value investing strategy, you can uncover hidden gems and seize opportunities that others may overlook. Embrace a forward-thinking mindset that embraces change and explores new avenues for value creation.

Paragraph 10: Exercising Caution and Due Diligence

While creativity and innovation are important, it's crucial to balance them with caution and due diligence. Value investing inherently involves risks, and it's essential to exercise caution when making investment decisions.

Avoid the temptation of speculative investments or "hot tips" that promise quick gains. Instead, focus on thorough research, data-driven analysis, and rational decision-making. Evaluate investments based on their long-term value potential and sustainability.

Maintain a margin of safety when selecting stocks, ensuring that the price you pay offers a significant discount to the intrinsic value. This provides a buffer against unforeseen market fluctuations and mitigates potential downside risks.

Continuously educate yourself and stay informed about the companies you invest in, industry trends, and broader economic conditions. Regularly review your portfolio and reassess your investment thesis. Be prepared to adjust your holdings if new information or changing market conditions warrant it.

Finally, consider seeking guidance from financial professionals or consulting with a trusted advisor. They can provide valuable insights, help you navigate complex investment decisions, and ensure that your investment strategy aligns with your financial goals and risk tolerance.

In conclusion

Value investing and utilizing P/E ratios present an opportunity to generate wealth and achieve long-term financial success. By incorporating creativity and innovation into your investment approach, while exercising caution and diligent risk management, you can navigate the value investing landscape with confidence. Stay disciplined, stay informed, and stay committed to your investment strategy as you work towards building a solid portfolio of value stocks.

Chapter 7: Make Money with Growth Stocks

Introduction:
Welcome to the exciting world of growth stocks, where the potential for substantial returns awaits those who are willing to embrace innovation and seek out promising investment opportunities. In this chapter, we will explore the steps you need to take to maximize your earning potential with growth stocks. From identifying promising companies to managing risks, we'll provide you with valuable insights to navigate this dynamic investment landscape.

Paragraph 1: Understanding Growth Stocks and Their Potential

Growth stocks are shares of companies that have demonstrated a history of strong and consistent revenue and earnings growth. These companies typically operate in rapidly expanding industries and offer innovative products or services that have the potential to disrupt traditional markets. Investing in growth stocks can be highly rewarding, as their rising earnings and market share often drive stock prices higher.

To fully grasp the potential of growth stocks, it's essential to understand their underlying drivers. Unlike value stocks, which are often undervalued based on their current financials, growth stocks derive their value from future growth prospects. Investors are willing to pay a premium for these stocks because they believe in the company's ability to deliver substantial revenue and earnings growth in the coming years. The key is to identify companies with a compelling growth story and a clear strategy to achieve their ambitious targets.

Paragraph 2: Identifying Promising Growth Companies

To identify promising growth companies, begin by researching industries with significant growth potential. Look for sectors that are experiencing technological advancements, changing consumer preferences, or emerging markets. For example, consider the renewable energy sector, where the shift toward clean energy sources presents ample opportunities for innovative companies.

Once you have identified a sector, analyze individual companies within it. Evaluate their financial performance, competitive advantages, and growth prospects. Look for companies with a track record of consistent revenue and earnings growth, strong management teams, and a solid business model. Additionally, consider their ability to adapt to changing market conditions and their commitment to innovation.

For instance, suppose you are interested in the electric vehicle (EV) industry. Research companies with a proven track record in EV manufacturing, a robust charging infrastructure, and a global market presence. Analyze their market share, product pipeline, and partnerships with key players in the industry. By delving deeper into their growth strategies, you can identify the companies with the greatest potential for future success.

Paragraph 3: Assessing Growth Potential

When evaluating growth stocks, it's essential to assess their growth potential. Look for companies with a compelling growth story supported by a clear strategy for expanding their market presence. Consider factors such as market size, addressable market opportunity, and competitive positioning. Companies with a unique value proposition, strong brand recognition, or disruptive technologies often have higher growth potential.

To illustrate, let's consider a hypothetical example of a software company that specializes in artificial intelligence (AI) applications. AI is a rapidly growing industry with immense potential for innovation across various sectors. Assess the company's technological expertise, the scalability of its products, and its ability to capitalize on emerging AI applications in industries such as healthcare, finance, or e-commerce. A company with a comprehensive growth strategy that addresses these factors is likely to have a higher growth potential.

Paragraph 4: Managing Risks Associated with Growth Stocks

While growth stocks offer the potential for substantial returns, they also come with inherent risks. It's crucial to manage these risks effectively. Diversify your portfolio by investing in a mix of growth stocks across different industries. This helps spread risk and minimizes the impact of any single investment's performance.

Additionally, conduct thorough due diligence and research before investing. Analyze a company's financial statements, industry trends, and competitive landscape. Evaluate potential risks such as competition, regulatory changes, and market volatility. Stay updated on company news and developments that may impact their growth trajectory.

For example, consider a hypothetical scenario where you are interested in investing in a biotechnology company focused on developing groundbreaking gene therapies. While the industry holds immense potential, it also faces regulatory uncertainties and the risk of clinical trial failures. To manage these risks, thoroughly research the company's pipeline of products, its partnerships with research institutions, and the expertise of its management team. Stay informed about regulatory updates and advancements in gene therapy technologies. By diversifying your portfolio across multiple growth stocks and staying vigilant about potential risks, you can better navigate the volatile nature of growth investments.

Paragraph 5: Investing with Caution

Investing in growth stocks requires caution and a long-term perspective. While it's tempting to chase short-term gains, focus on the company's long-term potential rather than short-term market fluctuations. Avoid making impulsive investment decisions based on speculative trends or rumors.

Instead, conduct thorough fundamental analysis to evaluate the company's financial health, growth prospects, and competitive advantages. Assess its valuation relative to its peers and industry benchmarks. Remember that investing in growth stocks often requires patience, as it may take time for the company's potential to materialize in the form of increased earnings and stock price appreciation.

Consider utilizing a dollar-cost averaging strategy, investing a fixed amount regularly, rather than trying to time the market. This approach allows you to mitigate the risk of investing large sums at unfavorable market conditions and take advantage of market downturns. By consistently investing over time, you can potentially benefit from compounding returns and reduce the impact of short-term market volatility.

Paragraph 6: Investing in High-Growth Sectors

High-growth sectors present unique opportunities for investors. For example, consider investing in companies involved in artificial intelligence, renewable energy, or biotechnology. These sectors have the potential for exponential growth due to increasing global demand, technological advancements, and evolving consumer preferences.

When investing in high-growth sectors, stay informed about industry trends and regulations. Monitor technological advancements and market dynamics that may impact the growth trajectory of companies within these sectors. Be prepared to adjust your portfolio as market conditions and industry landscapes evolve.

Additionally, consider the impact of sustainability and environmental, social, and governance (ESG) factors on high-growth sectors. Increasingly, investors are incorporating ESG considerations into their investment decisions. By investing in companies that prioritize sustainability, you can align your investment goals with broader societal and environmental objectives.

Paragraph 7: Growth Stocks as a Portfolio Component

Including growth stocks in your portfolio can enhance overall returns and diversify risk. However, it's important to strike the right balance between growth stocks and other asset classes, such as value stocks, bonds, and cash.

Diversification across different asset classes can help mitigate risk and reduce the impact of market volatility on your overall portfolio. Consider your investment objectives, risk tolerance, and time horizon when determining the appropriate allocation to growth stocks. Regularly review your portfolio and rebalance as necessary to maintain your desired asset allocation.

Conclusion:

Investing in growth stocks offers the potential for significant long-term returns. By understanding the dynamics of growth stocks, identifying promising companies within high-growth sectors, managing risks effectively, and investing with caution, you can maximize your opportunities for success. Remember to conduct thorough research, diversify your portfolio, and maintain a long-term perspective. With a creative and innovative approach to investing, coupled with diligent research and risk management, you can position yourself to make the most of the opportunities presented by growth stocks.

Chapter 8: Make Money with IPOs

Introduction:

Welcome to the exciting world of Initial Public Offerings (IPOs), where investors have the opportunity to participate in the early stages of a company's public journey and potentially reap significant financial rewards. In this chapter, we will explore the steps you need to take to maximize your chances of success when investing in IPOs. From understanding the IPO process to conducting thorough research, we'll provide you with valuable insights to navigate this unique investment opportunity.

Paragraph 1: Understanding IPOs and their Potential

An IPO occurs when a private company decides to go public by offering shares to the general public for the first time. It is an exciting milestone for a company as it provides access to public capital markets and offers investors the chance to own a piece of the company's future growth. IPOs can present an opportunity to invest in innovative and high-potential companies that may not have been accessible before.

Investing in IPOs requires careful consideration and due diligence. While there can be the potential for significant gains, it's important to approach these investments with caution. IPOs can be volatile, and there is always the risk of the stock price fluctuating significantly in the early stages of trading. It is crucial to evaluate the company's fundamentals, growth prospects, and industry dynamics before making investment decisions.

Paragraph 2: Researching IPO Candidates

When considering an IPO investment, start by researching the company's background, business model, and industry. Review the IPO prospectus, which provides detailed information about the company's financials, risks, and growth strategies. Pay attention to key metrics such as revenue growth, profitability, and competitive positioning. Look for companies with a unique value proposition, a strong management team, and a clear growth strategy.

To illustrate, let's consider a hypothetical technology company planning an IPO. Research its product offerings, market share, and competitive landscape. Analyze its financial statements and assess its ability to generate sustainable revenue growth. Consider factors such as customer demand, market size, and the company's potential for scalability.

Paragraph 3: Evaluating IPO Pricing and Valuation

Pricing is a critical factor to consider when investing in an IPO. The offering price is determined by the company and its underwriters based on market demand and company valuation. It's essential to evaluate the IPO pricing relative to the company's financial performance, growth potential, and industry benchmarks.

Consider the company's valuation multiples such as price-to-earnings (P/E) ratio, price-to-sales (P/S) ratio, and other relevant industry metrics. Compare these ratios with industry peers and historical IPO benchmarks. Keep in mind that a high valuation does not guarantee future success, and it's important to assess whether the company's growth prospects justify the price.

Paragraph 4: Assessing the IPO Roadshow and Investor Sentiment

During the IPO process, companies often conduct roadshows to promote their offering to potential investors. These roadshows provide an opportunity to learn more about the company's management team, business strategy, and growth prospects. Pay attention to how the company presents its story and addresses investor concerns during these presentations.

Evaluate investor sentiment surrounding the IPO. Assess the level of interest from institutional investors and the overall market demand for the offering. High demand can indicate positive market sentiment, but it's essential to consider whether the demand is driven by genuine confidence in the company's long-term potential or short-term speculative interest.

Paragraph 5: Timing and Allocation Strategy

Timing is crucial when investing in IPOs. Consider the overall market conditions and investor sentiment. An IPO in a favorable market environment with strong investor appetite for new offerings may increase the chances of a successful debut. However, be cautious of excessive hype and speculative behavior.

Develop an allocation strategy to manage your investment in IPOs effectively. Determine the amount you are willing to invest in IPOs and diversify your portfolio accordingly. It's advisable not to put all your capital into a single IPO but instead allocate funds across multiple offerings to spread the risk.

Consider participating in IPOs through various channels, such as brokerage firms, online platforms, or mutual funds specializing in IPO investments. Each channel may have different requirements, fees, and allocation methods. Research and choose the option that best suits your investment goals and risk tolerance.

Paragraph 6: Managing Risks and Setting Realistic Expectations

Investing in IPOs carries inherent risks, including market volatility and the potential for the stock price to deviate from the IPO price. It's crucial to set realistic expectations and understand that not all IPOs will experience immediate success.

Evaluate the company's competitive landscape, potential regulatory challenges, and the overall economic conditions that may impact its growth trajectory. Be prepared for potential price fluctuations and consider your investment horizon. It may take time for the company's fundamentals to materialize and for the stock price to reflect its true value.

To manage risks, consider setting stop-loss orders to protect against significant downside moves. This strategy allows you to automatically sell a portion or all of your shares if the stock price reaches a predetermined level. However, exercise caution with stop-loss orders as they can be triggered by short-term market volatility.

Paragraph 7: Long-Term Investment Approach

While IPOs can offer short-term trading opportunities, taking a long-term investment approach is often more advantageous. Look beyond the initial hype and focus on the company's growth potential over the coming years. Successful companies can deliver substantial returns to patient, long-term investors.

Consider companies that have a sustainable competitive advantage, a clear growth strategy, and a solid track record of execution. Evaluate their ability to generate consistent revenue and earnings growth, as well as their potential for market expansion and innovation.

An example of a successful IPO investment is a pharmaceutical company that has developed a breakthrough drug with significant market potential. Analyze the company's clinical trial data, regulatory approval progress, and market demand for the drug. Assess its ability to capture market share and generate long-term revenue growth.

Paragraph 8: Regular Portfolio Monitoring and Reassessment

Once you have invested in an IPO, it's crucial to regularly monitor the company's performance, industry trends, and any material changes in its fundamentals. Stay updated with news, earnings reports, and analyst opinions to make informed decisions about your investment.

Reassess your investment thesis periodically to ensure it aligns with the company's progress and evolving market conditions. Be prepared to adjust your investment strategy if there are significant changes in the company's prospects or if new investment opportunities arise.

Conclusion:

Investing in IPOs can be a rewarding but challenging endeavor. By conducting thorough research, evaluating pricing and valuation, managing risks, and adopting a long-term perspective, you can increase your chances of making profitable investments. Remember to diversify your portfolio, set realistic expectations, and stay informed about the companies and market dynamics. With a creative and innovative approach, combined with cautious decision-making, you can navigate the world of IPOs and potentially capitalize on exciting investment opportunities.

Chapter 9: How to Profit from a Stock That is Going Nowhere

Introduction:

In the dynamic world of stock market investing, not all stocks experience rapid price movements or upward trends. Sometimes, investors encounter stocks that seem to be stuck in a range, going nowhere in terms of significant price appreciation. However, even in such situations, there are strategies you can employ to potentially profit from these stocks. In this chapter, we will explore specific steps you can take to navigate and capitalize on opportunities presented by stocks that exhibit limited price movement. By employing creative and innovative approaches, while exercising caution, you can unlock the potential for profit in these seemingly stagnant stocks.

Paragraph 1: Understanding Stocks with Limited Price Movement

Stocks that are going nowhere refer to those that exhibit minimal or range-bound price fluctuations over an extended period. These stocks may lack a catalyst or significant market-moving news to drive substantial price changes. However, such stocks can still provide opportunities for profit by employing various strategies.

Investing in stocks that are going nowhere requires careful analysis and consideration. While the potential for rapid gains may be limited, these stocks may offer stability, consistent dividend payments, or potential value that has yet to be recognized by the market.

Paragraph 2: Conducting Thorough Fundamental Analysis

When identifying stocks that are going nowhere, it is crucial to conduct thorough fundamental analysis. Evaluate the company's financial health, including revenue, earnings, and cash flow trends. Assess the company's competitive position within its industry and analyze any potential catalysts for growth.

Look for stocks with solid fundamentals and a history of stable performance. Consider dividend-paying stocks, as consistent dividend payments can contribute to overall returns, even when price appreciation is limited.

For example, a utility company operating in a regulated market may exhibit limited price movement due to its stable and predictable earnings. However, its consistent dividend payments can still offer an attractive return on investment.

Paragraph 3: Identifying Potential Catalysts

While stocks that are going nowhere may lack immediate catalysts for significant price movements, identifying potential catalysts can uncover hidden opportunities. Look for upcoming company announcements, new product launches, or regulatory changes that could potentially impact the stock's price trajectory.

Consider the example of a pharmaceutical company with a pipeline of drugs in various stages of development. Even if the stock appears stagnant, the successful completion of a clinical trial or regulatory approval of a drug could trigger a substantial price increase.

Paragraph 4: Utilizing Options Strategies

Options strategies can provide innovative ways to profit from stocks that are going nowhere. Consider employing strategies such as selling covered calls or buying protective puts. Selling covered calls involves selling call options on stocks you already own, generating income from the premium received. Buying protective puts allows you to hedge against potential downside risk.

These options strategies can help generate income or limit potential losses, even if the stock price remains relatively unchanged.

For example, if you own 100 shares of a stock that is going nowhere, you could sell a covered call option with a strike price slightly above the current stock price. If the stock remains range-bound, you can continue collecting premiums from selling call options.

Paragraph 5: Implementing a Range-Trading Strategy

A range-trading strategy involves identifying key support and resistance levels within which a stock is trading. By buying near the support level and selling near the resistance level, you can potentially profit from the stock's price oscillations within the established range.

For example, if a stock consistently trades between $40 and $45, you can buy near $40 and sell near $45, aiming to capture the price movements within this range.

It's important to note that range-trading requires diligent monitoring of price levels and disciplined execution of buy and sell orders.

Paragraph 6: Employing Contrarian Investing Approaches

Contrarian investing involves taking positions opposite to prevailing market sentiment. When a stock is going nowhere, market sentiment may be pessimistic, creating potential buying opportunities.

Evaluate whether negative sentiment is unwarranted or overblown. Conduct in-depth research to identify undervalued stocks with strong fundamentals that may be overlooked by the market. By going against the crowd and investing in these undervalued stocks, you may position yourself for potential profit.

For example, if a stock is experiencing negative sentiment due to short-term challenges or market volatility, conduct a thorough analysis of its long-term growth prospects. If you believe the stock's fundamentals remain strong and the negative sentiment is temporary, consider accumulating shares at discounted prices.

Paragraph 7: Leveraging Technical Analysis Tools

In addition to fundamental analysis, technical analysis can provide valuable insights when dealing with stocks that are going nowhere. Use technical indicators and chart patterns to identify potential price reversals or breakout opportunities.

For instance, you can employ oscillators such as the Relative Strength Index (RSI) or Moving Average Convergence Divergence (MACD) to detect oversold or overbought conditions. Additionally, chart patterns like triangles, flags, or wedges can indicate potential price breakouts.

By combining technical analysis with fundamental analysis, you can make more informed decisions and increase the likelihood of profiting from stocks that are going nowhere.

Paragraph 8: Monitoring News and Market Trends

Stay updated on market news and trends that could impact the stocks you're targeting. Subscribe to financial news outlets, follow reliable market analysts, and monitor industry-specific developments.

News and events such as earnings reports, mergers and acquisitions, regulatory changes, or macroeconomic factors can influence a stock's trajectory, even if it has been stagnant. By staying informed, you can react quickly to potential opportunities or adjust your investment strategy accordingly.

Conclusion:

Profit opportunities exist even in stocks that appear to be going nowhere. By conducting thorough fundamental analysis, identifying potential catalysts, utilizing options strategies, implementing range-trading techniques, employing contrarian approaches, leveraging technical analysis tools, and monitoring market news and trends, you can increase your chances of profiting from these seemingly stagnant stocks.

Remember to exercise caution and manage risk appropriately. Diversify your portfolio to reduce exposure to any single stock, and always conduct thorough research before making investment decisions. With a creative and innovative mindset, combined with careful analysis and a disciplined approach, you can uncover hidden opportunities and potentially generate profits even in situations where stocks seem to be going nowhere.

Throughout the day, you stick to your trading plan, avoiding impulsive decisions and managing your emotions. You maintain discipline, following your risk management rules and focusing on high-probability setups.

At the end of the trading day, you review your trades, analyzing the outcomes and identifying areas for improvement. You learn from both successful and unsuccessful trades, refining your strategy and adapting to changing market conditions.

Remember, day trading requires practice and experience. It's essential to start with small position sizes and gradually increase as you gain confidence and proficiency. Never risk more than you can afford to lose, and always prioritize capital preservation.

Chapter 10: A Day Trading Strategy That Actually Works

Introduction:

Welcome to the exciting world of day trading, where quick decision-making and strategic execution can lead to profitable opportunities. In this chapter, we will explore a comprehensive day trading strategy that has proven to be effective in generating consistent profits. With a touch of creativity and innovation, we will dive into specific steps and examples to help you navigate this realm of financial markets with caution and maximize your earning potential.

Paragraph 1: Understanding the Market and Defining Your Trading Goals

To embark on a successful day trading journey, it is crucial to have a solid understanding of the market and define your trading goals. Study various asset classes, such as stocks, commodities, or forex, and identify which ones align with your trading style and preferences. Set realistic and achievable goals based on your risk tolerance, time commitment, and desired returns.

Paragraph 2: Conducting Thorough Technical Analysis

Technical analysis is a fundamental aspect of day trading. It involves studying price charts, patterns, and indicators to identify potential entry and exit points. Dive into the world of candlestick patterns, chart patterns like head and shoulders or double tops/bottoms, and popular indicators such as moving averages or relative strength index (RSI). By mastering technical analysis, you can enhance your ability to make well-informed trading decisions.

Paragraph 3: Utilizing Candlestick Patterns for Timing Entries

Candlestick patterns provide valuable insights into market sentiment and can help you time your entry and exit points more effectively. Examples of bullish candlestick patterns include engulfing patterns, morning stars, or hammer patterns, which indicate potential trend reversals or continuation. On the other hand, bearish patterns like shooting stars or evening stars suggest a possible trend reversal. By recognizing these patterns and their implications, you can optimize your trading entries.

Paragraph 4: Implementing a Robust Risk Management Strategy

Day trading involves inherent risks, and managing those risks is vital for long-term success. Implement a robust risk management strategy that includes determining your maximum risk per trade, setting stop-loss orders to limit potential losses, and using trailing stops to protect profits as the trade moves in your favor. Consistently adhering to your risk management plan will safeguard your capital and help you avoid significant drawdowns.

Paragraph 5: Identifying High-Volume and Volatile Stocks

In day trading, liquidity and volatility are key factors for potential profit opportunities. Focus on stocks with high trading volumes and price volatility, as these offer ample opportunities for quick trades and capturing price movements. Keep an eye on stocks that have breaking news, earnings announcements, or significant market events that can trigger substantial price fluctuations, allowing you to capitalize on the volatility.

Paragraph 6: Utilizing Market Depth and Level II Data

To gain a competitive edge in day trading, leverage market depth and Level II data. These tools provide insights into the supply and demand dynamics of a particular stock. Analyze bid-ask spreads, order sizes, and the presence of large buyers or sellers in the order book. By monitoring this information, you can make more informed trading decisions, identify potential entry and exit points, and gauge the overall market sentiment surrounding a stock.

Paragraph 7: Developing a Scalping Strategy for Quick Profits

Scalping is a popular day trading technique that involves capitalizing on small price fluctuations within a short period. Identify stocks with tight bid-ask spreads and execute quick trades to capture these small price movements. Scalping requires discipline, quick decision-making, and precise execution. Develop a scalping strategy based on your preferred time frame, risk tolerance, and the market conditions you are trading in.

Paragraph 8: Practicing Trade Journaling and Performance Review

Maintaining a trade journal and regularly reviewing your trading performance is essential for continuous improvement. Keep detailed records of your trades, including entry and exit points, reasons for the trade, trade duration, and the outcome. Additionally, record any emotions or observations during the trade. This journal will serve as a valuable tool for self-reflection and learning from both successful and unsuccessful trades. Regularly review your journal to identify patterns, strengths, weaknesses, and areas for improvement. By analyzing your trading performance, you can refine your strategy, adjust your risk management approach, and optimize your overall trading results.

Paragraph 9: Continuous Learning and Adaptation

In the dynamic world of day trading, continuous learning is crucial for staying ahead of the game. Keep yourself updated with the latest market trends, news releases, and economic indicators that can impact the stocks you trade. Stay informed about industry-specific developments, technological advancements, and emerging markets. Actively seek out educational resources such as books, courses, webinars, and seminars to expand your knowledge and refine your skills. Remember that adaptation is key—be open to adjusting your strategy as market conditions change and new opportunities arise.

Conclusion:

Mastering a successful day trading strategy requires a combination of market knowledge, technical analysis skills, effective risk management, and continuous learning. By understanding the market dynamics, conducting thorough technical analysis, utilizing candlestick patterns, implementing a robust risk management strategy, identifying high-volume and volatile stocks, utilizing market depth and Level II data, developing a scalping strategy, practicing trade journaling, and embracing continuous learning, you can increase your chances of success in day trading. Remember to approach day trading with caution, manage your risks effectively, and never stop refining your skills as you navigate the exciting and potentially rewarding world of day trading.

Chapter 11: Five Huge Mistakes That Beginners Make

Introduction:

Entering the world of investing can be both exciting and daunting for beginners. While the potential for financial gain is enticing, it's important to approach investments with caution and avoid common mistakes that can hinder your progress. In this chapter, we will explore five significant mistakes that beginners often make and provide specific steps to help you navigate these pitfalls with a touch of creativity and innovation. By understanding and avoiding these mistakes, you can maximize your investment opportunities while minimizing potential risks.

Paragraph 1: Lack of Research and Due Diligence

One of the most common mistakes beginners make is jumping into investments without conducting proper research and due diligence. It's essential to thoroughly understand the asset class or investment vehicle you're considering. Research the company's financials, growth prospects, competitive landscape, and industry trends. Look for potential risks, such as high debt levels or declining market share, and evaluate the investment's long-term potential before committing your funds. For example, if you're interested in investing in a technology company, dive into their product offerings, market position, and management team to assess their future growth prospects.

Paragraph 2: Emotional Decision-Making

Emotions can cloud judgment when it comes to investing. Avoid making impulsive decisions based on fear, greed, or short-term market fluctuations. Instead, develop a disciplined approach grounded in sound analysis and rational thinking. Stick to your investment plan and avoid making emotional decisions that can lead to costly mistakes. For instance, if a stock you own experiences a sudden drop in value, resist the urge to panic-sell and assess whether the company's fundamentals remain intact before making any decisions.

Paragraph 3: Lack of Diversification

Failing to diversify your investment portfolio is a significant mistake that can expose you to unnecessary risks. Spreading your investments across different asset classes, industries, and geographical regions can help mitigate the impact of any single investment's performance. Consider allocating your funds across stocks, bonds, real estate, and other investment vehicles to create a well-balanced portfolio. For example, if you have a significant portion of your portfolio in technology stocks, consider diversifying by investing in sectors such as healthcare, consumer goods, or utilities.

Paragraph 4: Chasing Quick Returns and Fads

Beginners often fall into the trap of chasing quick returns or investing in the latest fads without understanding the underlying fundamentals. While it's tempting to seek immediate gains, such investments often carry higher risks. Instead, focus on long-term investment strategies that align with your financial goals and risk tolerance. Invest in companies with solid fundamentals, sustainable growth prospects, and a track record of delivering value to shareholders. Avoid being swayed by short-term trends or hot investment tips that may not have a solid foundation.

Paragraph 5: Ignoring Risk Management

Effective risk management is crucial for successful investing. Beginners often overlook the importance of setting stop-loss orders, establishing risk-reward ratios, and determining the maximum amount they are willing to lose on a trade. Implementing proper risk management strategies helps protect your capital and ensures you can stay in the investment game for the long term. For instance, before entering a trade, define your risk tolerance and set a stop-loss order at a level that aligns with your risk management plan.

Paragraph 6: Overlooking the Power of Compounding

Compounding is a powerful tool for wealth creation, yet many beginners fail to take full advantage of it. By reinvesting dividends or returns into your portfolio, you can harness the power of compounding to accelerate your wealth accumulation over time. Don't underestimate the impact of consistent, long-term investing and the compounding effect it can have on your portfolio's growth. For example, if you receive dividend payments from your investments, consider reinvesting those dividends instead of taking

Paragraph 7: Neglecting Continuous Education

The world of investing is constantly evolving, and it's crucial for beginners to stay informed and continuously educate themselves. Take the time to read books, attend seminars, participate in online courses, and follow reputable financial news sources. By expanding your knowledge and understanding of various investment strategies, financial markets, and economic trends, you'll be better equipped to make informed decisions and adapt to changing market conditions. Consider joining investment clubs or online communities where you can exchange ideas and learn from experienced investors.

Paragraph 8: Failing to Maintain a Long-Term Perspective

Investing is a long-term game, and beginners often make the mistake of focusing on short-term fluctuations rather than the overall trajectory of their investments. It's essential to maintain a long-term perspective and avoid being swayed by temporary market volatility. Remember that successful investing requires patience, discipline, and a commitment to your financial goals. Avoid making impulsive decisions based on short-term market noise, and instead, focus on the underlying fundamentals and the long-term growth potential of your investments.

Paragraph 9: Seeking Professional Guidance

While it's important to take control of your investments, seeking professional guidance can be immensely valuable, especially for beginners. Consulting with a financial advisor or seeking the expertise of experienced investors can provide you with personalized advice, portfolio analysis, and guidance on investment strategies. A professional can help you navigate complex financial concepts, identify suitable investment opportunities, and provide objective insights during challenging market conditions. Consider engaging with a trusted advisor who aligns with your investment philosophy and understands your financial goals.

Conclusion:

By understanding and avoiding these five significant mistakes that beginners often make, you can enhance your investment journey and increase your chances of success. Conduct thorough research, make rational decisions, diversify your portfolio, focus on long-term strategies, implement effective risk management, harness the power of compounding, continuously educate yourself, maintain a long-term perspective, and seek professional guidance when needed. Remember, investing is a journey that requires patience, discipline, and a commitment to your financial goals. With the right mindset and a cautious approach, you can navigate the investment landscape creatively and innovatively, turning it into a fruitful opportunity for wealth accumulation.

Chapter 12: Insider Secrets of the Stock Market

Introduction:

The stock market is often perceived as a mysterious and complex world, with some investors seeming to possess insider knowledge that leads to their success. In this chapter, we will delve into the concept of "insider secrets" of the stock market, demystifying the notion and providing you with a creative and innovative approach to navigate this opportunity for financial gain. While we won't be discussing illegal insider trading, we will explore strategies and techniques that can give you an edge in the market. It's important to note that investments should be made with caution and adherence to legal and ethical guidelines.

Paragraph 1: Fundamental Analysis and Research

One of the key secrets to successful investing in the stock market is conducting thorough fundamental analysis and research. This involves evaluating a company's financial health, understanding its business model, assessing industry trends, and studying macroeconomic factors. By digging deep into the fundamentals, you can identify undervalued stocks with strong growth potential. For example, analyzing a company's financial statements, competitive position, and management team can provide valuable insights into its future prospects.

Paragraph 2: Technical Analysis and Chart Patterns

In addition to fundamental analysis, technical analysis can help you make informed investment decisions. By studying historical price patterns and market trends, you can identify potential entry and exit points. Chart patterns, such as support and resistance levels, trend lines, and moving averages, can provide visual cues for making trading decisions. For instance, recognizing a breakout from a bullish chart pattern may signal a buying opportunity.

Paragraph 3: Risk Management and Position Sizing

Successful investors understand the importance of effective risk management and position sizing. This involves setting stop-loss orders to limit potential losses, diversifying your portfolio across different asset classes, and determining the appropriate position size for each investment based on your risk tolerance. By managing risk effectively, you can protect your capital and ensure that no single investment has a significant impact on your overall portfolio.

Paragraph 4: Market Timing and Entry Points

Timing the market is a challenging task, but it can be a key factor in maximizing returns. By studying market trends, investor sentiment, and economic indicators, you can identify favorable entry points. For example, entering the market during periods of economic recovery or when specific sectors show strong growth potential may increase your chances of success.

Paragraph 5: Developing a Winning Strategy

Having a well-defined investment strategy is crucial for long-term success. It's important to align your strategy with your financial goals, risk tolerance, and time horizon. Whether you prefer value investing, growth investing, dividend investing, or a combination of strategies, developing a clear plan will help you stay focused and make consistent investment decisions.

Paragraph 6: Continual Learning and Adaptability

The stock market is constantly evolving, and successful investors understand the importance of continual learning and adaptability. Stay updated with the latest financial news, read books by renowned investors, attend seminars, and engage in online forums to expand your knowledge and refine your investment approach. Being adaptable and willing to adjust your strategies based on market conditions is key to staying ahead of the game.

Paragraph 7: Patience and Long-Term Perspective

Investing in the stock market requires patience and a long-term perspective. While short-term market fluctuations can be volatile, focusing on the long-term performance of your investments is essential. Warren Buffett, one of the most successful investors, famously said, "Our favorite holding period is forever." By maintaining a long-term perspective, you can ride out market volatility and potentially benefit from the compounding effect of long-term investment returns.

Paragraph 8: Managing Emotions and Avoiding Herd Mentality

One of the biggest challenges in stock market investing is managing emotions and avoiding the herd mentality. Emotions can cloud judgment and lead to impulsive decision-making, often resulting in poor investment choices. Fear and greed are two common emotions that can drive investors to make irrational decisions. Successful investors recognize the importance of keeping emotions in check and making decisions based on sound analysis and research.

To manage emotions effectively, it's essential to develop a disciplined approach to investing. This involves setting clear investment goals, creating a well-defined strategy, and sticking to predetermined rules. By having a plan in place, investors can resist the temptation to make impulsive trades based on short-term market fluctuations.

Avoiding herd mentality is another crucial aspect of successful investing. When investors follow the crowd and make investment decisions based on popular opinion, they often overlook the underlying fundamentals of a company or the market. This can lead to buying at inflated prices during market peaks or selling at rock-bottom prices during market downturns.

Successful investors understand the importance of independent thinking and conducting thorough research. They focus on analyzing company financials, industry trends, and market conditions to make informed decisions. By relying on their own analysis rather than following the crowd, they can uncover undervalued opportunities and avoid overhyped investments.

Furthermore, it's important to stay informed and avoid being swayed by sensationalist news or market rumors. Conducting diligent research and relying on credible sources of information can help investors make rational decisions based on facts rather than emotions.

Practicing mindfulness and self-awareness can also be beneficial in managing emotions. By recognizing and acknowledging emotions as they arise, investors can take a step back, assess the situation objectively, and make rational decisions based on their investment strategy.

In conclusion, managing emotions and avoiding herd mentality are essential skills for successful stock market investing. By developing a disciplined approach, conducting independent research, staying informed, and practicing mindfulness, investors can make rational decisions and increase their chances of achieving long-term financial success.

Paragraph 9: Harnessing the Power of Technology and Data

In today's digital age, technology plays a significant role in stock market investing. Utilize cutting-edge tools and platforms that provide real-time market data, research reports, and analytical tools. Leverage the power of data analytics to identify trends, patterns, and opportunities that may not be apparent to the naked eye. By harnessing technology and data, you can make more informed investment decisions and stay ahead of the competition.

Paragraph 10: Building a Network and Seeking Mentorship

Building a network of like-minded individuals and seeking mentorship can provide valuable insights and guidance. Attend industry events, join investment clubs, and connect with experienced investors who can share their knowledge and experiences. A mentor can provide guidance, offer different perspectives, and help you navigate through challenging situations. Surrounding yourself with knowledgeable and supportive individuals can enhance your learning and growth as an investor.

Conclusion:

By exploring the insider secrets of the stock market, you have gained valuable insights into the strategies and techniques that can give you an edge in your investment journey. Remember to conduct thorough research, leverage fundamental and technical analysis, manage risk effectively, time your entries, develop a winning strategy, continually learn and adapt, maintain a long-term perspective, manage emotions, utilize technology and data, and build a network of supportive individuals. Approach investments with caution and adhere to legal and ethical guidelines. With a creative and innovative mindset, you can navigate the stock market with confidence and increase your chances of financial success.

Chapter 13: From Small Beginners to Great Wealth

Introduction:

Welcome to the captivating journey of transforming from a small beginner to achieving great wealth through strategic investments. In this chapter, we will explore a comprehensive set of steps and techniques to help you navigate this path with creativity, innovation, and cautiousness. By following these principles, you can maximize your investment opportunities and witness substantial growth in your wealth. Let's delve deeper into the strategies that can pave the way to financial success.

Paragraph 1: Defining Your Financial Goals

Begin by meticulously defining your financial goals. Take the time to identify your aspirations, whether it's securing a comfortable retirement, purchasing a dream home, or establishing a solid foundation for your children's future. By setting specific, measurable, attainable, relevant, and time-bound (SMART) goals, you can develop a clear roadmap for your investment journey.

Paragraph 2: Assessing Your Risk Tolerance

Understanding your risk tolerance is vital before making any investment decisions. Every individual possesses a unique comfort level when it comes to taking risks. Evaluate your capacity to handle volatility and align your investments accordingly. Remember, higher potential returns often correlate with higher levels of risk.

Paragraph 3: Building a Diversified Portfolio

The key to managing risk and maximizing returns lies in constructing a well-diversified portfolio. Distribute your investments across various asset classes, industries, and geographical regions. This approach helps mitigate the impact of any individual investment's performance on your overall portfolio.

Paragraph 4: Conducting In-Depth Investment Research

Conduct thorough research on potential investment opportunities to identify those that align with your goals and risk tolerance. Explore stocks, bonds, mutual funds, exchange-traded funds (ETFs), real estate, and other investment vehicles. Utilize both fundamental analysis, evaluating a company's financials and competitive position, and technical analysis, studying market trends and patterns, to make informed investment decisions.

Paragraph 5: Embracing a Long-Term Perspective

Adopting a long-term perspective is crucial when it comes to investment success. Short-term market fluctuations can trigger uncertainty and anxiety, potentially leading to impulsive decision-making. Instead, focus on the underlying fundamentals of your investments and their long-term growth potential. Avoid being swayed by short-term market movements.

Paragraph 6: Regular Portfolio Reviews and Adjustments

Regularly review your portfolio to ensure it remains aligned with your goals and risk tolerance. As your circumstances change or market conditions evolve, you may need to rebalance your investments or adjust your asset allocation. Stay informed about market trends, economic indicators, and geopolitical events to make informed decisions.

Paragraph 7: Optimizing Tax-Efficient Strategies

Explore tax-efficient investment strategies to maximize your returns. Take advantage of tax-advantaged accounts such as Individual Retirement Accounts (IRAs) or 401(k) plans, where contributions and growth may be tax-deferred or tax-free. Additionally, consider tax-loss harvesting, a strategy to offset capital gains with capital losses, reducing your overall tax liabilities.

Paragraph 8: Seeking Professional Guidance

Consider seeking professional advice from financial advisors or wealth managers. These experts provide personalized guidance based on your unique financial situation, goals, and risk tolerance. They can offer expertise, monitor your investments, and help you navigate complex financial landscapes, ensuring you make well-informed decisions.

Paragraph 9: Embracing Innovation and Emerging Trends

Stay abreast of emerging trends and technological advancements in the investment world. Explore opportunities in sectors such as renewable energy, artificial intelligence, biotechnology, and other innovative industries. Embrace the potential of disruptive technologies to uncover new investment avenues and capitalize on their growth potential.

Paragraph 10: Practicing Patience, Discipline, and Continuous Learning

Patience, discipline, and continuous learning are paramount on the path to great wealth. To further enhance your journey, consider the following additional steps:

Paragraph 11: Cultivating a Savings Habit

Develop a disciplined savings habit to fuel your investment endeavors. Set aside a portion of your income regularly, even before considering investments. This practice not only provides you with a safety net but also increases the capital available for investment opportunities.

Paragraph 12: Network and Collaborate

Engage with like-minded individuals in investment communities, forums, or local groups. Networking allows you to share ideas, gain insights from experienced investors, and potentially collaborate on investment opportunities. Collaborative efforts can lead to diversification and shared knowledge, strengthening your overall investment strategy.

Paragraph 13: Keep Up with Economic Indicators

Stay informed about key economic indicators such as GDP growth, inflation rates, interest rates, and employment figures. Understanding the broader economic landscape can help you make more informed investment decisions and identify sectors that are poised for growth.

Paragraph 14: Harness the Power of Compounding

Take advantage of the power of compounding by reinvesting your investment returns. By reinvesting dividends, interest, or capital gains, you can accelerate the growth of your portfolio over time. Compounding allows your investments to generate additional earnings, creating a snowball effect of wealth accumulation.

Paragraph 15: Adopt a Mindful Approach

Practice mindfulness in your investment journey. Avoid making impulsive decisions driven by fear or greed. Instead, approach each investment with a calm and rational mindset. Take the time to thoroughly analyze potential risks and rewards before making any investment decisions.

Paragraph 16: Stay Educated and Adaptable

Continuously educate yourself about investment strategies, market trends, and financial news. Attend seminars, read books, follow reputable financial publications, and consider online courses to expand your knowledge base. The investment landscape evolves, and staying adaptable is key to making informed decisions.

Paragraph 17: Seek Multiple Income Streams

Consider diversifying your income streams beyond traditional investments. Explore additional avenues such as side businesses, rental properties, or online ventures. Having multiple sources of income can provide stability and enhance your overall financial position.

Paragraph 18: Practice Risk Management

Implement effective risk management techniques in your investment approach. Set stop-loss orders to limit potential losses, use trailing stops to protect profits, and diversify your investments to spread risk. Understanding and managing risk is essential to safeguarding your wealth.

Conclusion:

From small beginnings to great wealth, your journey requires dedication, discipline, and a well-structured approach. Define your financial goals, assess your risk tolerance, build a diversified portfolio, conduct thorough research, embrace a long-term perspective, regularly review and adjust your investments, optimize tax-efficient strategies, seek professional guidance, embrace innovation, practice patience and discipline, cultivate a savings habit, network and collaborate, stay informed about economic indicators, harness the power of compounding, adopt a mindful approach, stay educated and adaptable, seek multiple income streams, and practice risk management. Remember, investing is a continuous learning process, and success comes to those who remain committed to their financial goals and adapt to changing market conditions.

Conclusion:

As we wrap up this journey from small beginners to great wealth, it's important to approach investing with a touch of levity and prudence. While the financial markets can be exciting and filled with potential, they also demand careful consideration and a balanced perspective.

Remember, investing is not a get-rich-quick scheme but a long-term endeavor. It requires patience, discipline, and a clear understanding of your financial goals. By following thr steeps throughout the book, you can navigate the complexities of the investment world with confidence.

But let's not forget to enjoy the process along the way. Investing doesn't have to be a dry and serious pursuit. Embrace the excitement of discovering new opportunities, the thrill of seeing your investments grow, and the camaraderie of engaging with fellow investors.

As you embark on your investment journey, keep in mind the lessons we've discussed: define your goals, diversify your portfolio, conduct thorough research, stay informed, adapt to change, and manage risk. But also remember to smile, appreciate the small victories, and learn from the inevitable challenges that come your way.

So, my fellow investors, go forth with optimism and a sprinkle of humor. Be oculate in your investment decisions, seizing opportunities while maintaining a cautious eye. Trust your instincts, seek knowledge, and embrace the ever-evolving nature of the financial markets.

May your investments flourish, your wealth grow, and your financial dreams become a reality. And above all, enjoy the journey and savor the satisfaction of turning small beginnings into great success.

Happy investing!

Printed by Libri Plureos GmbH in Hamburg, Germany